Market to Millions

The Ultimate Directory to Free eBook Promotion

By David A. Ogren

Market to Millions: The Ultimate Directory to FREE eBook Promotion

Copyright © 2016 David A. Ogren

Images courtesy of zirconicusso at FreeDigitalPhotos.net

If you have any questions about the directory (additions, errors, etc.), please contact me directly at: mrkt2millions@gmail.com

Table of Contents

Introduction

Writing a book is both an incredibly challenging process and a rewarding experience. Just consider your circuitous path to authorship. You had a great idea that morning over your bagel and coffee and thought, "I should write a book about bagels and coffee!". Or, perhaps you are a Cleveland Browns fan and decided to self-medicate by writing on the psychology of depression and franchise loyalty.

You may have researched for months, wrestled with outlines, written multiple drafts and edited until your puffy eyes were exhausted. Now, the book is done and you can finally relax.... well, that was fun for a minute. Now, you realize that people should know about your book, read it, and recommend it to others. After completing my first book some months ago, this was the stage in which I found myself.

I soon recognized that the real work was getting people to know my book existed, then purchase it. Like most of you, my marketing campaign fund might buy the Grande Meal at Taco Bell, but it was not going to turn many heads. When I started to search around for cheap alternatives, I stumbled upon multiple websites claiming to have lists of places that will market my eBook for free by listing it with their website, blog, twitter followers, newsletter, or daily email. However, when I attempted to follow the links, many took me to obsolete pages, old domain names, or places that now charged for advertising.

Frustrated with that process, I began building my own list of vetted sites that were live, currently accepting book submissions, and providing a chance for my book to get some downloads. This directory does not purport to provide a master class in eBook marketing techniques (there are plenty of those!), but simply provides an advertising database that gives you over 150 places to market your eBook for $0. That's not a bad start. Some of the sites are quite small and focused, while others are massive behemoths of potential. Whatever your topic, you will likely find some great options for marketing your eBook.

I have organized the sites alphabetically and itemized the web address, marketing niche, global site ranking, category ranking, estimated visitors per month, and direct link to submit your book. These parameters give some basic information that will help you decide if that site is a good option for you. Collectively, there are at least 66.5 Million visitors to these sites each month (not including Facebook and Reddit profiles). Even if you average that number to a daily amount, then multiply only by 5 Kindle promotion days, you still get over 11 Million potential visitors over those 5 days…. decent product exposure on the budget of $0.

Near the end of the book, I have a chart that lists the top 40 sites by visitors per month. It is a nice tool to see the data in a different light.

It is time to begin marketing your great idea to the masses!

If you have any questions about the directory (or additions, errors, etc.), please contact me directly at:

mrkt2millions@gmail.com

A

All You Can Books

Website: http://www.allyoucanbooks.com

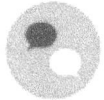

Niche: Unlimited eBooks to subscription base

Global Website Rank: 88,904

Category Rank (Books/Literature - eBooks): 68

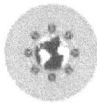

Visits per Month: 577,200

How to Submit your eBook:

email book details to yurym@allyoucanbooks.com

Ana E Meyer

Website: http://anaemeyer.blogspot.com/

Marketing Niche: Book Reviews

Global Website Rank: 21,208,514

Category Rank (Books/Literature - eBooks): n/a

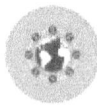

Visits per Month: 235

How to Submit your eBook:
http://anaemeyer.blogspot.com/p/review-policy.html

Armadillo eBooks

Website: http://www.armadilloebooks.com/

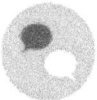

Marketing Niche: Free/Discounted eBooks

Global Website Rank: 4,262,610

Category Rank (Arts and Entertainment): 380,420

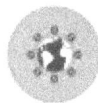

Visits per Month: 3,400

How to Submit your eBook:
http://www.armadilloebooks.com/submit-free-ebooks/

Ask David

Website: http://askdavid.com/

Niche: Author resources, Free eBooks for readers

Global Website Rank: 1,195,550

Category Rank (Books and Literature): 3,313

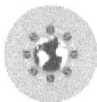

Visits per Month: 17,700

How to Submit your eBook:
http://askdavid.com/free-ebook-promotion

Awesome Gang

Website: http://awesomegang.com/

Marketing Niche: Features books and authors on multiple platforms/categories

Global Website Rank: 1,557,645

Category Rank (Adult): 58,602

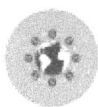

Visits per Month: 12,200

How to Submit your eBook:
http://awesomegang.com/submit-your-book/

B

BeeZee Books

Website: http://beezeebooks.com

Marketing Niche: Author and reader resources

Global Website Rank: 2,331,207

Category Rank (Books and Literature): 5,855

Visits per Month: 3,700

How to Submit your eBook:
http://beezeebooks.com/blogging/

Best eBooks World

Website: http://www.bestebooksworld.com/

Marketing Niche: Free eBook directory

Global Website Rank: 1,644,731

Category Rank (Books and Literature): 4,323

Visits per Month: 12,900

How to Submit your eBook:
http://www.bestebooksworld.com/contactus.asp

Binge on Books

Website: http://bingeonbooks.com/

Marketing Niche: Book reviews

Global Website Rank: 8,856,363

Category Rank (Books and Literature): n/a

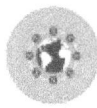

Visits per Month: 1,000

How to Submit your eBook:
http://bingeonbooks.com/submit-your-book-for-review/

Book Angel

Website: http://bookangel.co.uk/

Marketing Niche: Free and 0.99 eBooks

Global Website Rank: 3,331,528

Category Rank (Arts and Entertainment): 299,845

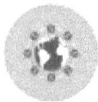

Visits per Month: 3,800

How to Submit your eBook:
http://bookangel.co.uk/submit-a-book/

Book Bongo

Website: http://bookbongo.com/

Marketing Niche: Free and discounted books

Global Website Rank: 6,167,192

Category Rank (Internet and Telecom): 7,404

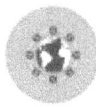

Visits per Month: 1,900

How to Submit your eBook:
http://bookbongo.com/submit/

Book Circle, The

Website: http://book-circle.com/

Marketing Niche: Free and discounted books

Global Website Rank: 10,204,289

Category Rank (Publishing and Printing): 12,477

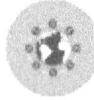

Visits per Month: 656

How to Submit your eBook:

http://book-circle.com/submit-free-kindle-ebook-listing/

Book Deal Hunter

Website: http://bookdealhunter.com/

Marketing Niche: Books sent to subscribers

Global Website Rank: 4,845,324

Category Rank (Publications): 4,548

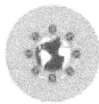

Visits per Month: 2,000

How to Submit your eBook:
http://bookdealhunter.com/submit-free-book/

Book Hitch

Website: http://www.bookhitch.com/

Marketing Niche: Provides a book search engine

Global Website Rank: 12,134,005

Category Rank (Publications): 9,678

Visits per Month: 266

How to Submit your eBook: Login and create free listing. http://www.bookhitch.com/login.aspx

Book Hippo

Website: http://bookhippo.uk/

Marketing Niche: Sends daily book bargains

Global Website Rank: 1,086,940

Category Rank (Publications): n/a

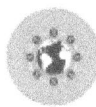

Visits per Month: 15,300

How to Submit your eBook: Create author page, then list a new release under "author tools"

Book House of Mysteries and Thrillers

Website: http://www.book-house-of-mysteries-and-thrillers.com/

Marketing Niche: Author promotions for mysteries and thrillers

Global Website Rank: 17,823,588

Category Rank (Publications): n/a

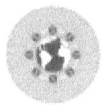

Visits per Month: 235

How to Submit your eBook: http://www.book-house-of-mysteries-and-thrillers.com/services.html

Book of the Day

Website: http://bookoftheday.org

Marketing Niche: Author promotion, book lists

Global Website Rank: 4,631,251

Category Rank (Books and Literature): n/a

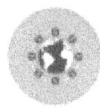

Visits per Month: 3,200

How to Submit your eBook:
http://bookoftheday.org/add-book/

Book Pleasures

Website: http://www.bookpleasures.com

Marketing Niche: Book reviews and interviews

Global Website Rank: 5,279,961

Category Rank (Books and Literature): 11,983

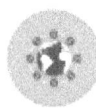

Visits per Month: 2,400

How to Submit your eBook:
http://www.bookpleasures.com/websitepublisher/categorie
s/Book-Review-Submission-Guidelines/

Book Pinning

Website: http://bookpinning.com

Marketing Niche: Online board for authors

Global Website Rank: 4,049,536

Category Rank (Books and Literature): 3,879

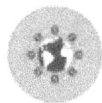

Visits per Month: 2,600

How to Submit your eBook:
http://bookpinning.com/?sws=home/submit-book

Book Praiser

Website: http://bookpraiser.com

Marketing Niche: Connects readers and authors

Global Website Rank: 4,244,429

Category Rank (Publishing and Printing): 5,079

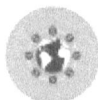

Visits per Month: 1,600

How to Submit your eBook:
http://bookpraiser.com/login/?redirect_to=http://bookpraiser.com/listyourbook/

Book Preview Club

Website: http://bookpreviewclub.com/home/

Marketing Niche: Author discovery and promotion

Global Website Rank: 7,330,206

Category Rank (Arts and Entertainment): 641,301

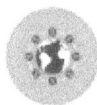

Visits per Month: 874

How to Submit your eBook:
http://bookpreviewclub.com/thank-you-free/

Book Talk

Website: http://www.booktalk.org/

Marketing Niche: Forums, links, advertising

Global Website Rank: 516,298

Category Rank (Books and Literature): 1,613

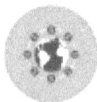

Visits per Month: 27,400

How to Submit your eBook: Create an account, then post a new thread in desired forum

Book Tour Tips

Website: http://www.booktour.tips/

Marketing Niche: Author resources, promotions

Global Website Rank: 29,237,368

Category Rank (A and E): 2,454,825

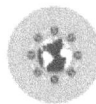

Visits per Month: 77

How to Submit your eBook:
http://www.booktour.tips/list-your-free-bargain-pre-order-book/

Bookworm World

Website: https://www.bookwormworld.com/

Marketing Niche: eBook reviews, promotion deals

Global Website Rank: 27,263,289

Category Rank (Video Games): 148,207

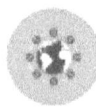

Visits per Month: 98

How to Submit your eBook:
https://www.bookwormworld.com/contact-us.html

C

Content Mo

Website: http://contentmo.com/

Marketing Niche: eBook ads, blogs, social media

Global Website Rank: 8,817,060

Category Rank (Business and Industry): 1,660,496

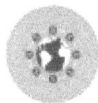

Visits per Month: 1,000

How to Submit your eBook:
http://contentmo.com/submit-your-free-ebook-promo

Choosy Bookworm

Website: https://choosybookworm.com/

Marketing Niche: Featured books, eBook newsletters, daily deals, free books

Global Website Rank: 1,379,554

Category Rank (Arts and Entertainment): 128,941

Visits per Month: 20,500

How to Submit your eBook:
https://choosybookworm.com/free-ebook-promotion/

Christian Book Readers

Website: http://christianbookreaders.com/

Marketing Niche: Book newsletters and author services for Christian titles

Global Website Rank: 5,523,847

Category Rank (People and Society): 111,139

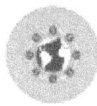

Visits per Month: 1,200

How to Submit your eBook:
http://christianbookreaders.com/submit-your-free-books/

Christian Kindle News

Website: http://christiankindlenews.com/

Niche: Free eBooks and deals for Christian titles

Global Website Rank: 4,937,646

Category Rank (People and Society): 98,666

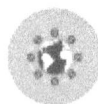

Visits per Month: 3,100

How to Submit your eBook:
http://christiankindlenews.com/submit-free-christian-ebook-deal/

D

Daily Bookworm, The

Website: http://thedailybookworm.com/

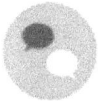

Marketing Niche: Bookstore, reviews, resources

Global Website Rank: 11,090,561

Category Rank (Arts and Entertainment): 18,132

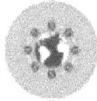

Visits per Month: 523

How to Submit your eBook:
http://thedailybookworm.com/submit-free-books2/

Debut City

Website: http://www.debutcity.com/Home.htm

Marketing Niche: Book debuts, deals, reviews

Global Website Rank: 34,984,438

Category Rank (Arts and Entertainment): n/a

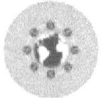

Visits per Month: 33

How to Submit your eBook:
http://www.debutcity.com/Submit.htm

Digital Book Today

Website: http://digitalbooktoday.com/

Marketing Niche: Connecting authors and readers

Global Website Rank: 708,080

Category Rank (Books and Literature): 2,108

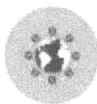

Visits per Month: 60,600

How to Submit your eBook:
http://digitalbooktoday.com/join-our-team/12-top-100-submit-your-free-book-to-be-included-on-this-list/

Discount Book Man

Website: http://digitalbooktoday.com/

Marketing Niche: Free eBooks, multiple categories

Global Website Rank: 12,314,474

Category Rank (Business and Industry): 308,595

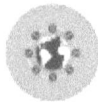

Visits per Month: 450

How to Submit your eBook:
http://discountbookman.com/book-promotion/

E

eBookasaurus

Website: http://ebookasaurus.com/

Marketing Niche: eBook daily deals, to subscribers

Global Website Rank: 5,365,255

Category Rank (Business and Industry): 12,176

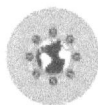

Visits per Month: 1,800

How to Submit your eBook:
http://ebookasaurus.com/free-book-listing/

eBook Hounds

Website: http://www.ebookhounds.com/

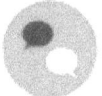

Niche: Free, discounted books to subscribers

Global Website Rank: 1,380,404

Category Rank (Business and Industry): 198,578

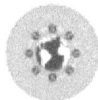

Visits per Month: 28,600

How to Submit your eBook:
http://www.ebookhounds.com/books/submit/

eBookLister

Website: http://ebooklister.net/

Niche: Free, bargain eBooks by indie authors

Global Website Rank: 2,445,309

Category Rank (Business and Industry): 2,457

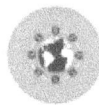

Visits per Month: 5,000

How to Submit your eBook:
http://ebooklister.net/submit.php

eBooks Habit

Website: http://ebookshabit.com/

Marketing Niche: Free and bargain eBooks

Global Website Rank: 1,623,286

Category Rank (Publications): 1,679

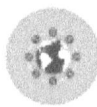

Visits per Month: 11,500

How to Submit your eBook:
http://ebookshabit.com/for-authors/

eReader Cafe

Website: http://theereadercafe.com/

Marketing Niche: Bargain and Free Kindle eBooks

Global Website Rank: 395,810

Category Rank (Publications): 1,230

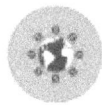

Visits per Month: 100,800

How to Submit your eBook:
http://theereadercafe.com/promote-your-books/

eReader Girl

Website: http://ereadergirl.com/

Marketing Niche: eBook deals, free and discounted, author of the week.

Global Website Rank: 3,334,166

Category Rank (Publications): 176,383

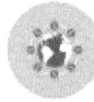

Visits per Month: 3,900

How to Submit your eBook:
http://ereadergirl.com/submit-your-ebook/

Every Writer

Website: http://www.everywritersresource.com/

Niche: Advertising, classifieds, book promotion

Global Website Rank: 255,346

Category Rank (Books and Literature): 844

Visits per Month: 167,300

How to Submit your eBook:
http://everywritersresource.com/selfpublished/submit-your-book/

F

Facebook Groups

Website: http://facebook.com

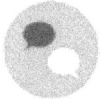

Marketing Niche (for our purposes): Social groups that encourage author sharing/book promotion

Global Website Rank: 1

Category Rank (Social Network): 1

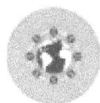

Visits per Month: Data not available to specific groups

How to Submit your eBook: Join group, then submit your book info. Creating your own page is, of course, a great tool itself.

The Kindle Publishing Bible:
https://www.facebook.com/groups/KindlePublishers/

Amazon Kindle Publishers' Group:
https://www.facebook.com/groups/kindleauthors/

Book Marketing:
https://www.facebook.com/groups/bookmarketing/

Authors Promoting Authors:
https://www.facebook.com/groups/apablog/

Free Books:
https://www.facebook.com/groups/270558336379692/

Free eBooks Download:
https://www.facebook.com/groups/126278657527255/

FREE books R Us:
https://www.facebook.com/groups/freebkrus/

Free Today on Amazon:
https://www.facebook.com/groups/FreeTodayOnAmazon/

Free E Books:
https://www.facebook.com/groups/215918835174776/

Free eBooks:
https://www.facebook.com/groups/1013820968756497/

Free Kindle Books:
https://www.facebook.com/groups/426282137432533/

Free E-Books:
https://www.facebook.com/groups/freeebooks/

Free Ebooks for Kindle, Nook, and More:
https://www.facebook.com/groups/341840249197060/

Crazy for books (readers and authors):
https://www.facebook.com/groups/182637088529255/

Awesome Free Kindle Books Here!:
https://www.facebook.com/groups/294455560643884/

Free & Bargain Books from The Daily Bookworm:
https://www.facebook.com/groups/Dailybookworm/

Share FREE eBooks:
https://www.facebook.com/ShareFreeeBooks/

Kindle Reviews:
https://www.facebook.com/groups/567675336598902

KDP Select Authors - Kindle Unlimited Readers:
https://www.facebook.com/groups/KDPSelectAuthors/

Amazon Kindle Book Reviews:
https://www.facebook.com/groups/bookpromos/

The Fab Friday 99 Cents Promotion Group for Authors:
https://www.facebook.com/groups/fabfridaypromo

Book Reviews & Promotion & Suggestions:
https://www.facebook.com/groups/366603943499492/

Kindle REVIEW Exchange Group:
https://www.facebook.com/groups/KindleReviewExchange

Amazon Book Reviews:
https://www.facebook.com/groups/327748523911323/

The Book Authors Club:
https://www.facebook.com/groups/1497696577118959/

Free Kindle Books and Great Deals:
https://www.facebook.com/groups/444613228885288

Bookaholics:
https://www.facebook.com/groups/141612599209928

Promote Your Books:
https://www.facebook.com/groups/429650897189445/

Kindle e Books - Free - $2.99:
https://www.facebook.com/groups/1577441379149696/

EbooksNBooksPromosGroup:
https://www.facebook.com/groups/eBooksBooksPromo

Promote Your Book!:
https://www.facebook.com/groups/promote.your.book.here/

All Things Books:
https://www.facebook.com/groups/236837269664074

Book Junkie Promotions:
https://www.facebook.com/groups/bookjunkiepromotions/

The Literary Lounge authors, writers, publishers, and illustrators:
https://www.facebook.com/groups/135486133130440/

Books: https://www.facebook.com/groups/books45/

Kindle Publishers:
https://www.facebook.com/groups/512098985483106/

2 friends, promote your books with us:
https://www.facebook.com/groups/2friendspromatewithauthors

Book Promotion:
https://www.facebook.com/groups/BookPromotion

Passion for Books:
https://www.facebook.com/groups/passionforbooks/

Support an Author:
https://www.facebook.com/groups/supportanauthor/

Authors 99¢ e-Books Promotion:
https://www.facebook.com/groups/444695995585913/

Julies Book Review- Reviewers for Authors:
https://www.facebook.com/groups/JBRauthorpage/

BOOK PROMOTION:
https://www.facebook.com/groups/725631810822368

Amazon Book Clubs:
https://www.facebook.com/groups/AmazonBookClubs/

Amazon book and eBook readers:
https://www.facebook.com/groups/419504758165134/

Authors Promoting Authors:
https://www.facebook.com/groups/apablog

Book Lovers:
https://www.facebook.com/groups/2204565182

Book Reviews & Promotion:
https://www.facebook.com/groups/148313988694907/

BOOK REVIEW & PROMOTION:
https://www.facebook.com/groups/bookpromo.review/

Authors, Reviewers, & Book Lovers:
https://www.facebook.com/groups/BooksLuvers

Online Book Publicity Group:
https://www.facebook.com/groups/online.book.publicity/

Writers and Readers Unite:
https://www.facebook.com/groups/69073710111/

Amazon Kindle Book Sharing Club:
https://www.facebook.com/groups/kindlebooksharingclub

Kindle Krazy! Authors Actively Seeking Readers:
https://www.facebook.com/groups/241846582600572/

Kindle ...: https://www.facebook.com/groups/acrebooks/

Kindle Review Exchange 5 Stars:
https://www.facebook.com/groups/KindleReviewExchange5Stars

Kindle Free/Cheap Books:
https://www.facebook.com/groups/114270575327081

Book promotions:
https://www.facebook.com/groups/623206594363552

Faithful Reads

Website: http://faithfulreads.com/

Marketing Niche: Affordable Christian eBooks

Global Website Rank: 773,092

Category Rank (People and Society): 11,740

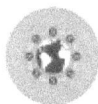

Visits per Month: 49,000

How to Submit your eBook:
http://faithfulreads.com/authors/

Free 99 Books

Website: http://www.free99books.com/

Niche: Free and 99c books, indie authors

Global Website Rank: 5,829,691

Category Rank (Books and Literature): n/a

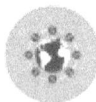

Visits per Month: 1,500

How to Submit your eBook:
http://www.free99books.com/author/add

Freebies 4 Mom

Website: http://freebies4mom.com/

Marketing Niche: Deals, prizes and freebies

Global Website Rank: 512,908

Category Rank (Coupons): 906

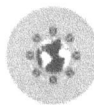

Visits per Month: 82,000

How to Submit your eBook:
https://docs.google.com/forms/d/e/1FAIpQLScwGpTVqE3k7
T2pEGEq0rV7ve42PVHjawbCoGS7D-
yYrW58pA/viewform?embedded=true&formkey=dGktOG5x
bEZDYVVBUFE1S21DZUxoeFE6MQ

Free Book Club

Website: http://www.freebookclub.org/

Niche: Free Kindle eBooks, author advertising

Global Website Rank: 4,963,635

Category Rank (Publications): 11,360

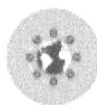

Visits per Month: 1,500

How to Submit your eBook:
http://www.freebookclub.org/awpcp/place-ad/

Free Books

Website: http://www.freebooks.com/

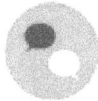

Marketing Niche: Free eBooks and textbooks

Global Website Rank: 448,907

Category Rank (Books and Literature): 1,432

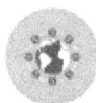

Visits per Month: 69,800

How to Submit your eBook:
http://www.freebooks.com/submit/

Free eBooks Blog

Website: http://www.freeebooksblog.com/

Marketing Niche: Bargain and free Kindle books

Global Website Rank: 2,605,697

Category Rank (Books and Literature): 6,425

Visits per Month: 8,300

How to Submit your eBook:
http://www.freeebooksblog.com/contact/

Free Kindle Books

Website: http://www.free-kindle-books-4u.com/

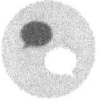

Niche: Free books lists, author promotion

Global Website Rank: 1,501,517

Category Rank (Arts and Entertainment): 139,857

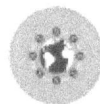

Visits per Month: 9,400

How to Submit your eBook: http://www.free-kindle-books-4u.com/promote-your-book/

Free Online Novels

Website: http://www.free-online-novels.com/

Marketing Niche: Links to free books

Global Website Rank: 383,876

Category Rank (Books and Literature): 1,233

Visits per Month: 90,900

How to Submit your eBook: http://www.free-online-novels.com/submissions.html

Free Stuff Times

Website: http://www.freestufftimes.com/

Marketing Niche: Free items online, coupons, contests, hot deals

Global Website Rank: 102,977

Category Rank (Coupons): 263

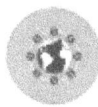

Visits per Month: 434,400

How to Submit your eBook:
http://www.freestufftimes.com/about-the-site

Frugal Freebies

Website: http://www.frugal-freebies.com/

Marketing Niche: Free eBooks, coupons, giveaways

Global Website Rank: 2,309,439

Category Rank (Coupons): 2,269

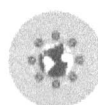

Visits per Month: 9,300

How to Submit your eBook: http://www.frugal-freebies.com/p/submit-freebie.html

G

Get Free eBooks

Website: http://www.getfreeebooks.com/

Niche: Author promotions, guest writing, tips

Global Website Rank: 95,630

Category Rank (Books and Literature/E Books): 70

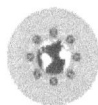

Visits per Month: 542,400

How to Submit your eBook:
http://www.getfreeebooks.com/submit-your-ebooks/

Good Reads

Website: https://www.goodreads.com/

Marketing Niche: Author and reader resources, book lists, quizzes, trivia

Global Website Rank: 397

Category Rank (Books and Literature): 3

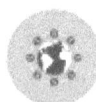

Visits per Month: 90,100

How to Submit your eBook:

http://www.goodreads.com/author/program

https://www.goodreads.com/topic/show/1605420-post-your-kindle-countdown-deal-here

H

Hunt 4 Freebies

Website: http://hunt4freebies.com/

Marketing Niche: Coupons, freebies, sweepstakes

Global Website Rank: 57,777

Category Rank (Coupons): 161

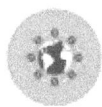

Visits per Month: 928,200

How to Submit your eBook:
http://hunt4freebies.com/submit-freebie

Human Made

Website: http://www.humanmade.net/

Niche: Free books and author promotions

Global Website Rank: 14,288,881

Category Rank (Coupons): 1,226,852

Visits per Month: 472

How to Submit your eBook:
http://www.humanmade.net/submission-form

I Love eBooks

Website: http://www.iloveebooks.com/

Niche: Kindle daily deals, giveaways, advertising

Global Website Rank: 4,941,314

Category Rank (Publications): 11,314

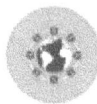

Visits per Month: 2,600

How to Submit your eBook:
http://www.iloveebooks.com/for-authors.html

Indie Book Lounge

Website: http://indiebooklounge.com/

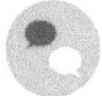

Niche: Site tailored to indie authors and their books

Global Website Rank: 8,080,225

Category Rank (Adult): 199,868

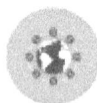

Visits per Month: 889

How to Submit your eBook: Register, then add your book. http://indiebooklounge.com/register.php

Indie Book of the Day

Website: http://indiebookoftheday.com/

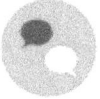

Marketing Niche: Author blurbs, reviews, book club, free kindle books

Global Website Rank: 4,213,285

Category Rank (Books and Literature): 9,863

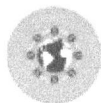

Visits per Month: 3,400

How to Submit your eBook:
http://indiebookoftheday.com/authors/free-on-kindle-listing/

Indies Unlimited

Website: http://www.indiesunlimited.com/

Marketing Niche: Blog, book promos, advertising, bookstore, resources

Global Website Rank: 656,355

Category Rank (Books and Literature): 1,972

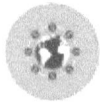

Visits per Month: 59,200

How to Submit your eBook:
http://www.indiesunlimited.com/freebie-friday/thrifty-thursday/

It's Write Now

Website: http://itswritenow.com/

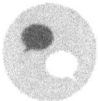

Niche: Free eBooks, bargain books, testimonials

Global Website Rank: 5,806,994

Category Rank (Books and Literature): 13,053

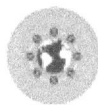

Visits per Month: 2,200

How to Submit your eBook:
http://itswritenow.com/submit-your-book/

Ipen Designs

Website: http://ipendesigns.net/

Marketing Niche: Book reviews, bookstore

Global Website Rank: n/a

Category Rank (Books and Literature): n/a

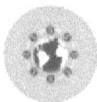

Visits per Month: unknown

How to Submit your eBook: (for book review)
http://ipendesigns.net/reviews/

J

Just Free and Bargain Books

Website: http://justfreeandbargainbooks.com/

Marketing Niche: Bargain books in multiple categories, advertising for all authors

Global Website Rank: 24,615,725

Category Rank (Books and Literature): n/a

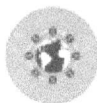

Visits per Month: 170

How to Submit your eBook:
http://justfreeandbargainbooks.com/daily-update-submissions/

K

Kobo

Website: https://www.kobo.com/

Marketing Niche: eBooks, magazines, apps, eReaders, free eBooks

Global Website Rank: 58,703

Category Rank (Books and Literature - eBooks): 53

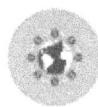

Visits per Month: 938,400

How to Submit your eBook:
https://www.kobo.com/writinglife

K on the Cheap

Website: https://konthecheap.wordpress.com/

Marketing Niche: Daily deals, fire deals

Global Website Rank: 17,222,877

Category Rank (Shopping): 1,069,603

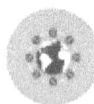

Visits per Month: 251

How to Submit your eBook:
https://konthecheap.wordpress.com/contact/

Korner Konnection

Website: http://kornerkonnection.com/

Niche: Reciprocal promotion through Facebook

Global Website Rank: 5,375,304

Category Rank (Publishing and Printing): 6,469

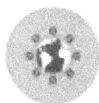

Visits per Month: 2,000

How to Submit your eBook:
http://kornerkonnection.com/

Kindle Book Promos

Website:http://kindlebookpromos.luckycinda.com/

Marketing Niche: Free eBooks, countdown deals, new releases, author resources

Global Website Rank: n/a

Category Rank (Publishing and Printing): n/a

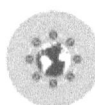

Visits per Month: 1,500

How to Submit your eBook:
http://kindlebookpromos.luckycinda.com/?page_id=283

Kindle Book Review

Website: http://kindlebookreview.net/

Marketing Niche: Book reviews from readers

Global Website Rank: 12,274,071

Category Rank (Marketing/Advertising): 307,346

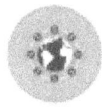

Visits per Month: 516

How to Submit your eBook:
http://kindlebookreview.net/submitfreebook.html

http://form.jotform.com/21078469493969

Library Thing

Website: https://www.librarything.com/

Niche: Community of readers and authors

Global Website Rank: 20,727

Category Rank (Reference, Libraries): 14

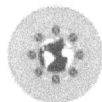

Visits per Month: 2,100

How to Submit your eBook: Register, then post new thread https://www.librarything.com/talk

Lovely Books

Website: http://lovelybookpromotions.com/

Niche: Free eBooks, promotions, blog, audiobooks

Global Website Rank: 3,290,269

Category Rank (Reference, Libraries and Museums): 296,248

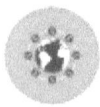

Visits per Month: 3,500

How to Submit your eBook:
http://lovelybookpromotions.com/submit-your-kindle-freebie/

M

My Book Cave

Website: https://mybookcave.com/

Marketing Niche: Book reviews, book deals based on content ratings

Global Website Rank: 688,432

Category Rank: n/a

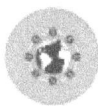

Visits per Month: 32,800

How to Submit your eBook: Login, then submit book. http://mybookcave.com/submit-book/

My Book Place

Website: http://mybookplace.net/

Niche: Book features, giveaways, author interviews

Global Website Rank: 4,986,706

Category Rank: n/a

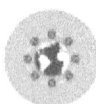

Visits per Month: 2,300

How to Submit your eBook:
http://mybookplace.net/submit-your-book/

N

New Free Kindle Books

Website: http://newfreekindlebooks.com/

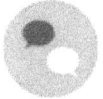

Marketing Niche: Free eBooks, book reviews, book deals, eBook promotion

Global Website Rank: 4,779,993

Category Rank (Business and Industry): 842,943

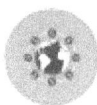

Visits per Month: 2,900

How to Submit your eBook:
http://newfreekindlebooks.com/authors/

O

One Hundred Free Books

Website: https://ohfb.com/

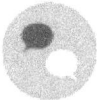

Niche: Top Kindle deals, discounted/free eBooks

Global Website Rank: 170,545

Category Rank (Internet and Telecom): 1,046

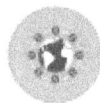

Visits per Month: 180,100

How to Submit your eBook:
https://ohfb.com/book-sale-notice/

P

People Reads

Website: http://www.peoplereads.com/

Niche: eBook deals delivered to your inbox

Global Website Rank: 5,816,454

Category Rank (Internet and Telecom): 513,211

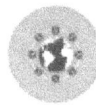

Visits per Month: 1,800

How to Submit your eBook:
http://www.peoplereads.com/list-your-ebook

Pretty Hot

Website: http://pretty-hot.com/

Marketing Niche: eBook newsletter, author interviews and advertising, featured books

Global Website Rank: 8,044,568

Category Rank (Internet and Telecom): 199,300

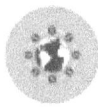

Visits per Month: 1,200

How to Submit your eBook: http://pretty-hot.com/submit-your-book/

R

Reader's Favorite

Website: https://readersfavorite.com/

Marketing Niche: Awards and book reviews

Global Website Rank: 974,935

Category Rank (Books and Literature): 2,800

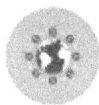

Visits per Month: 15,600

How to Submit your eBook:
https://readersfavorite.com/book-reviews.htm

Readers in the Know

Website: http://www.readersintheknow.com/home

Marketing Niche: Book podcast, blog, subscribers are notified of the chosen promotions

Global Website Rank: 1,771,291

Category Rank (Books and Literature): 163,786

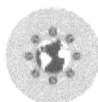

Visits per Month: 8,700

How to Submit your eBook:
http://www.readersintheknow.com/publisher/promos/new

Read Freely

Website: http://www.readfree.ly/

Marketing Niche: Discounted and free eBooks

Global Website Rank: 2,658,322

Category Rank (Books and Literature): n/a

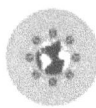

Visits per Month: 5,900

How to Submit your eBook:
http://www.readfree.ly/submityourfreebook/

Reading Deals

Website: http://readingdeals.com/

Niche: Free/discounted eBooks sent to inbox daily

Global Website Rank: 2,667,601

Category Rank (Coupons): 2,477

Visits per Month: 8,900

How to Submit your eBook:
http://readingdeals.com/submit-ebook/free

Read Write Club

Website: http://www.readwriteclub.com/

Niche: Featured books, author interviews, ads

Global Website Rank: n/a

Category Rank (Coupons): n/a

Visits per Month: unknown

How to Submit your eBook:
http://www.readwriteclub.com/submit-your-book/

Reddit Groups

Website: http://www.reddit.com

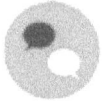

Niche: Social groups for authors, books releases

Global Website Rank: 27

Category Rank (Social Media): 6

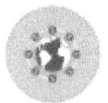

Visits per Month: Data n/a for specific groups

How to Submit your eBook:

https://www.reddit.com/r/wroteabook/

https://www.reddit.com/r/eFreebies/submit

https://www.reddit.com/r/FreebooksforKindle/submit

https://www.reddit.com/r/FreeEBOOKS/submit

https://www.reddit.com/r/selfpublish/

https://www.reddit.com/r/ebooks/

Riffle Select

Website: https://www.rifflebooks.com/

Niche: Featured books for readers, book discovery

Global Website Rank: 697,214

Category Rank (Publications): 767

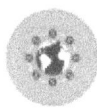

Visits per Month: 51,300

How to Submit your eBook:
https://www.rifflebooks.com/advertise/get-started

S

Slick Deals

Website: https://slickdeals.net/

Niche: Online shopping, deals, forums, deal alerts

Global Website Rank: 857

Category Rank (Coupons): 2

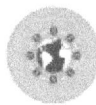

Visits per Month: 59,400,000

How to Submit your eBook: Login, then create new thread in Free Digital goods
https://slickdeals.net/forums/forumdisplay.php?f=54

Smashwords

Website: https://www.smashwords.com/

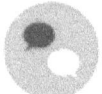

Marketing Niche: Publish eBooks, over 350,000 eBooks for readers, online store

Global Website Rank: 17,928

Category Rank (Books and Literature, eBooks): 18

Visits per Month: 2,100,000

How to Submit your eBook:
https://www.smashwords.com/about/how_to_publish_on_smashwords

Story Finds

Website: http://storyfinds.com

Niche: Author spotlight, daily specials, blog, ads

Global Website Rank: 2,637,881

Category Rank (Arts and Entertainment): 239,370

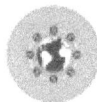

Visits per Month: 5,300

How to Submit your eBook: email promo@storyfinds.com and ask to be listed on the Free Reads page.

http://storyfinds.com/promotions-for-authors

Star Book Reviews

Website: http://www.starbookreviews.com

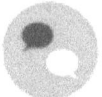

Niche: Book reviews provided and rated by readers

Global Website Rank: n/a

Category Rank (Arts and Entertainment): n/a

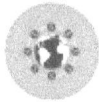

Visits per Month: unknown

How to Submit your eBook:
http://www.starbookreviews.com/submit/

Totally Free Stuff

Website: http://www.totallyfreestuff.com

Niche: Free items under multiple categories

Global Website Rank: 137,337

Category Rank (People and Society): 4,057

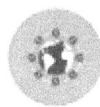

Visits per Month: 276,100

How to Submit your eBook:
http://www.totallyfreestuff.com/submit.asp

Top Book Reviewers

Website: http://www.topbookreviewers.com/

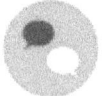

Marketing Niche: Reviews for books and eBooks

Global Website Rank: 36,305,876

Category Rank (Books and Literature): 63,152

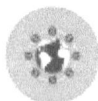

Visits per Month: 18

Submit your eBook: Login, then list your book.
http://www.topbookreviewers.com/index.php?url=authors/author_info/

U

Uncustomary Book Review, The

Site: http://www.uncustomarybookreview.com/

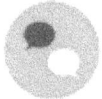

Marketing Niche: Book reviews, featured authors, book submissions

Global Website Rank: 8,502,015

Category Rank (Books and Literature): 18,083

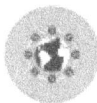

Visits per Month: 1,100

How to Submit your eBook:
http://www.uncustomarybookreview.com/book-submission/

W

Wall of Books, The

Website: http://www.thewallofbooks.com/

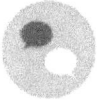

Marketing Niche: Book listings for all authors

Global Website Rank: 14,257,876

Category Rank (Online Marketing): 43,939

Visits per Month: 318

How to Submit your eBook:
http://www.thewallofbooks.com/register/

Writers Net

Website: http://www.writers.net/

Niche: Resources, forums for writers and authors

Global Website Rank: 700,945

Category Rank (Books and Literature): 2,083

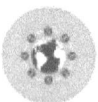

Visits per Month: 39,900

How to Submit your eBook:
http://www.writers.net/user/create.php

Y

Your Daily eBooks

Website: http://www.yourdailyebooks.com/

Niche: Listings for popular and free eBooks

Global Website Rank: 2,765,389

Category Rank (Social Network): 6,360

Visits per Month: 8,400

How to Submit your eBook:
http://www.yourdailyebooks.com/sample-page/

Z

Zwoodle Books

Website: http://zwoodlebooks.com/

Niche: Reviews, daily specials, author lists

Global Website Rank: 18,454,830

Category Rank (Publications): 13,359

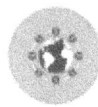

Visits per Month: 310

How to Submit your eBook:
http://zwoodlebooks.com/authors-and-publishers/

Top 40 Websites by Average Monthly Visitors

	Website	Monthly Visitors
1	Slickdeals	59,400,000
2	Smashwords	2,100,000
3	https://www.kobo.com/writinglife	938,400
4	http://hunt4freebies.com/submit-freebie	928,200
5	http://www.allyoucanbooks.com/contact	577,200
6	http://getfreeebooks.com/submit-your-ebooks/	542,400
7	http://www.freestufftimes.com/	434,400
8	http://www.totallyfreestuff.com/submit.asp	276,100
9	http://ohfb.com/book-sale-notice/	180,100
10	EveryWritersResource	167,300
11	http://theereadercafe.com/promote-your-books/	100,800
12	http://www.free-online-novels.com/submissions.html	90,900
13	http://goodreads.com/author/program	90,100
14	http://Freebies4Mom	82,000
15	http://freebooks.com/submit/	69,800

16	DigitalBookToday	60,600
17	IndiesUnlimited	59,200
18	http://rifflebooks.com/advertise/get-started	51,300
19	http://faithfulreads.com/authors/	49,000
20	http://www.writers.net/forum/forum.php	39,900
21	http://mybookcave.com/submit-book/	32,800
22	http://www.ebookhounds.com/books/submit/	28,600
23	BookTalk	27,400
24	https://choosybookworm.com/free-ebook-promotion/	20,500
25	http://askdavid.com/free-ebook-promotion	17,700
26	http://readersfavorite.com/book-reviews.htm	15,600
27	http://bookhippo.uk/	15,300
28	http://www.bestebooksworld.com/addlinks.asp	12,900
29	http://awesomegang.com/submit-your-book/	12,200
30	http://ebookshabit.com/for-authors/	11,500
31	FreeKindleBooks4U	9,400
32	http://frugal-freebies.com/p/submit-freebie.html	9,300
33	http://readingdeals.com/submit-ebook/free	8,900

34	ReadersInTheKnow	8,700
35	http://www.yourdailyebooks.com	8,400
36	http://freeebooksblog.com/contact/	8,300
37	http://www.readfree.ly/submityourfreebook/	5,900
38	https://storyfinds.com/promotions-for-authors	5,300
39	http://ebooklister.net/submit.php	5,000
40	http://ereadergirl.com/submit-your-ebook/	3,900

Thanks!

Wow, you made it through! Congratulations on your new book launch. I hope this directory was helpful and that it simplified the process of marketing your book to millions of people for $0.

Would you take 30 seconds and review my eBook on Amazon? I would greatly appreciate it!

If you have any questions about the directory (additions, errors, etc.), please contact me directly at:

mrkt2millions@gmail.com